What???
No subscription to
Scifaikuest??

We can fix that . . .

https://www.hiraethsffh.com/product-page/scifaikuest-1

Or get a sample back issue to check us out!

https://www.hiraethsffh.com/shop-1

And a subscription makes a great gift, for a holiday or any time of the year!

Minimalism:
A Handbook of Minimalist Genre Poetic Forms

This handbook contains articles about how to write various minimalist poetry forms such as scifaiku, senryu, sijo, haibun, empat perkataan, ghazals, cinquain, cherita, rengays, rengu, octains, tanka, threesomes, and many more. Each article is written by an expert in that particular poetry form.

Teri Santitoro, aka sakyu, who assembled this handbook, has been the editor of Scifaikuest since 2003.

https://www.hiraethsffh.com/product-page/minimalism-a-handbook-of-minimalist-genre-poetic-forms

A Little Help, Please

In the world of the small indie press we fight a never-ending battle for attention to our work, as writers and in publishing. Here's an example: big publishers [you know who they are] have gobs of $$$ that they can devote to advertising and marketing. Here at Hiraeth Publishing, our advertising budget consists of the deposits for whatever soda bottles and aluminum cans we can find alongside the highways. Anti-littering laws make our task even more difficult . . . ☺

That's where YOU come in. YOU are our best promoter. YOU are the one who can tell others about us. Just send 'em to our website, tell them about our store. That's all. Just that.

Of course, we don't mind if you talk us up. We're pretty good, you know. We have some award-winning and award-nominated writers and artists, plus other voices well-deserving to be heard [not everyone wins awards, right?] but our publications are read-worthy nevertheless.

That number once again is:
www.hiraethsffh.com

Friend us on Facebook at Hiraeth Publishing

Follow us on Twitter at @HiraethPublish1

SCIFAIKUEST
November 2023

6	A Little Help, Please
8	Editorial
10	Skeletal Knight by Greg Fewer
11	The Roxanne Barbour Page
12	The Deborah Karl-Brandt Page
13	The Lorelyn de La Cruz Arevalo Page
14	The Randall Andrews Page
15	The David C. Kopaska-Merkel Page
16	The Dylan Mabe Page
17	The Michael P Coglan Page
18	The DJ Tyrer Page
19	The Lee Strong, OFC Page
20	The Stephen C. Curro Page
21	The Tyler McIntosh Page
22	The John Hawkhead Page
23	The Simon Kewin Page
24	The Benjamin Whitney Norris Page
25	Scifaiku
31	Tanka & Other Minimalist Forms
32	Headache Cure by Denise Noe
38	Haibun
44	Article: Through by Robert E. Porter
49	Featured Poet: Joshua St. Claire
53	Interview: Joshua St. Claire
56	t.santitoro: my favorite poem
58	Who's Who

THE STAFF OF SCIFAIKUEST:
TERI SANTITORO, EDITOR

SCIFAIKUEST is published quarterly online and in print. The two editions are different.

Cover art "Zombie Soldier" by John Hawkhead
Cover design by Laura Givens

Vol. XXI, No. 2   November 2023
Scifaikuest [ISSN 1558-9730] is published quarterly on the 1st day of February, May, August, and November in the United States of America by Hiraeth Publishing, P.O. Box 1248, Tularosa, NM 88352. Copyright 2023 by Hiraeth Publishing. All rights revert to authors and artists upon publication. Nothing may be reproduced in whole or in part without written permission from the authors and artists. Any similarity between places and persons mentioned in the fiction or semi-fiction and real places or persons living or dead is coincidental. Writers and artists guidelines are available online at
https://www.hiraethsffh.com/scifaikuest.
Guidelines are also available upon request from Hiraeth Publishing, P.O. Box 1248, Tularosa, NM, 88352, if request is accompanied by a SASE #10 envelope with a first-class US stamp. Subscriptions: $28 for one year [4 issues], $44 for two years [8 issues]. Single copies $9.00 postage paid in the United States. Subscriptions to Canada: $33 for one year, $51 for two years. Single copies $11.00 postage paid to Canada. U.S. and Canadian subscribers remit in U.S. funds. All other countries inquire about rates.

SALE!!

There's a sale going on!! It's still going on!!

All the books you can order at 20% off the total! Woot!

Buy 1 book; buy 100 books! It's all the same discount. Use the code **BOOKS2023** (after 1 Jan 24 use **BOOKS2024)** when you check out.

Go to the Shop at www.hiraethsffh.com and make those selections now!

You'll be glad you did. So will we.

EDITORIAL

Welcome and Happy Halloween!

I'm hoping you had a wonderfully spooky holiday and are now looking forward to a less scary but equally fun Thanksgiving!

Our delightfully creepy COVER is *Zombie Soldier,* by **John Hawkhead.** And we also have FIVE interior illustrations: *headache cure* by **Denise Noe**, *Martian Landscape3* by **ARPY,** *fibonobservation* by **James Kotsyba**r, *Through* by **ARPY,** and *Skeletal Knight* by **Greg Fewer**!

Scifaikuest now has it's own ISBN!!! Please inform your local book stores and library that they are now able to ORDER SCIFAIKUEST!!!

You can now find us at Hiraeth Books at:
https://www.hiraethsffh.com/home-1

If you don't have a subscription to our PRINT edition, they are available at:
https://www.hiraethsffh.com/product-page/scifaikuest

And, if you would like to join the select group of contributors by submitting your poetry, artwork or article, you can find our guidelines at:
https://www.hiraethsffh.com/scifaikuest

You can also read our ONLINE VERSION at:
https://www.hiraethsffh.com/scifaikuest-online

Pssst! Looking for something to read?

You can get **t.santitoro's** newest novel, *Those Who Die,* at:
THOSE WHO DIE by t. santitoro | Hiraeth Publishing (hiraethsffh.com)

You can order **t.santitoro's** latest novella, *Adopted Child,* at:
https://www.hiraethsffh.com/product-page/adopted-child-by-t-santitoro

You can also get a copy of her novelette, *The Legend of Trey Valentine,* at:
https://www.hiraethsffh.com/product-page/legend-of-trey-valentine-by-teri-santitoro

I guess we're still growing because, as always, we'd love to extend a huge *Scifaikuest* "Welcome!" to our many newest contributors: **Randall Andrews**, **Jenelle Clausen, Michael Coglan, Lorelyn De la Cruz Arevalo,** Deborah Karl-Brandt, **Richard L. Matta,** and **Christina Nordlander!**

through abundant treats
the thing at the bag's bottom
extending a tentacle

(xeno-unit)

Skeletal Knight
Greg Fewer

The Roxanne Barbour Page

aroma of space
dirty socks
death

ahead of time
first step
future

gazing
through spaceship portholes
micrometeorites

Mars
solitary dune
dreaming of waves

The Deborah Karl-Brandt Page

hibernation...
deep inside the cocoons
little aliens

witching hour...
the books starts
to whisper

new born lambs ...
the shadow of a flying dragon
lowers his head

cleared area...
the couple´s chainsaw with
too much red on it

The Lorelyn de la Cruz Arevalo Page

a hiker
leaving no trace —
quick sand

full moon —
human again
he hides from the pack

the wolf
sewn on its skin
her father's clothes

new neighbors...
a replica
of us

The Randall Andrews Page

canine abductions
evil thieving aliens
steal our happiness

snakes in the cockpit
specters in the cargo hold
space sickness is real

wolfman unemployed
uninsured and off his meds
lock your doors tonight

vampire volunteer
Red Cross receptionist
perfect penance

The David C. Kopaska-Merkel Page

leather armchair
the head on the wall
bares its fangs

she spreads legs
and arms after jumping
ripcord in my hand

chalk flowers bloom
on limestone walls behind me
mammoths charge

love letters
inscribed on my exes' skin
returned unopened

The Dylan Mabe Page

in the sea of space
the ethereal tail whips
our ship back to Earth

interstellar trip
Little Boy and a cat food bag
personal items

I want a front porch
a mandolin on the moon
lunar hillbilly

The Michael P Coglan Page

I leap
waiting to feel gravity --
wrong planet

a messy ship --
the tiny robot
chirps to life

leaving Earth --
our ancestors
failed us

The DJ Tyrer Page

black cat
witch's familiar
steals nine more lives

security job
patrolling haunted building
never return home

lost hospital
vile experiments
horror unleashed

The Lee Strong, OFS Page

at his sentencing
vampire grows even paler -
life without parole

researcher turns on
interdimensional door -
Who's that knocking?

blind date takes
unexpected turn
her tattoos moves

The Stephen C. Curro Page

interstellar hub
like clockwork
starships coming and going

spaceport diner
pilots swap
solar system gossip

the strange flash
of antimatter
containment breach

The Tyler McIntosh Page

a spasm
in my bicep
rewiring

data security training
I scour memory chips
at the morgue

scrubbing rust
I stroke the cheek
that still feels

The John Hawkhead Page

blood feud
along the husk's carcase
hieroglyph wounds

first contact
a pulse of three sixes
from the black hole

opening the crypt
a line of footsteps
scorched on stone

The Simon Kewin Page

baby newly born
silently it watches you
eyes that flame with red

doll with china face
shiny wide smile unblinking
it whispers your name

moonlit night at sea
ship's bell tolling in the fog
no hands hold the wheel

The Benjamin Whitney Norris Page

last op
that dark cloud above?
a chipped obsidian blade
for our vivisection

for the birds
debased and bedeviled
the hunter's blind
a grouse pecked out his eyes

Ashley
How I love to see her
stripped down to the bare wood
and kneeling in my fireplace

cold turkey
leaving me
without a leg to stand on
best drumstick I ever tasted

SCIFAIKU

"Trick of Treat"
wizard of oz costume
cloak and pointy hat
not to be used in rain

    Matthew Wilson

"September Shade"
cooler autumn temperature
after blazing summer
only 15 kelvin

    Matthew Wilson

climbing the spine
of a calcified god
crippled city

    Daniel Gene Barlekamp

shipwrecked Lunar tardigrades -
dead or
alive?

    Lauren McBride

Halloween night
costumed pet owners
walking their werewolves

    Guy Belleranti

her alien eyes
always burning with passion
many hearts melted

    Guy Belleranti

summer memories
the scent of freshly mowed
cemetery

    Richard L. Matta

Mars' red sand sparkles
the long departed's stain
silent testimony

    Colleen Anderson

I wake up
from dreams of desert sands –
fresh tan on my skin

    Christina Nordlander

Pan
the faint brittle snap
of twigs under cloven hooves
a horned shadow falls

    Josh Maybrook

Pious Folk
faithfully bringing
all their tithes to the chapel
even their firstborn

    Josh Maybrook

headlines tell parents
warn children against swimming
in acid flowers

    Jenelle Clausen

two headed creature
still mourning
death of left head

    Denny E. Marshall

harvest moon
the scarecrow's grin
grows wider

    Ngo Binh Anh Khoa

alien earworms
slowly devouring my brain
till it turns to mush

    Ngo Binh Anh Khoa

ancient vampire sleeps
fanged dentures on nightstand
soaking in red wine

    Gabriel Smithwilson

post-apocalypse
biting into last Twinkie
I taste cockroach blood

    Gabriel Smithwilson

detectives find out
skeletons at factory
not made of plastic

    Denny E. Marshall

diamond in the rough
finding her finger
in beach sand

    Richard L. Matta

shivering brass bell
black death silences voices
sorrow's song a river

    Colleen Anderson

strange footsteps echo upstairs
a missing axe
then screams of discovery

    Brian Rosenberger

the witches market
shelves of dead familiars
quivering for a new coven

    Brian Rosenberger

driving in the rain
the lady in white beckons
I don't dare to look

    Brian Barnett

they came from the sky
leathery wings and talons
swooping and snatching

    Brian Barnett

collected treasures
in a rack over the fire
drying tongues still hiss

Ronnie Smart

broken pentagram
limbs hanging from the rafters
you shouldn't have called

Ronnie Smart

CINQUAIN

monster

monster
free, ferocious
calculating, plotting
relishing its own fine weirdness
human

Denise Noe

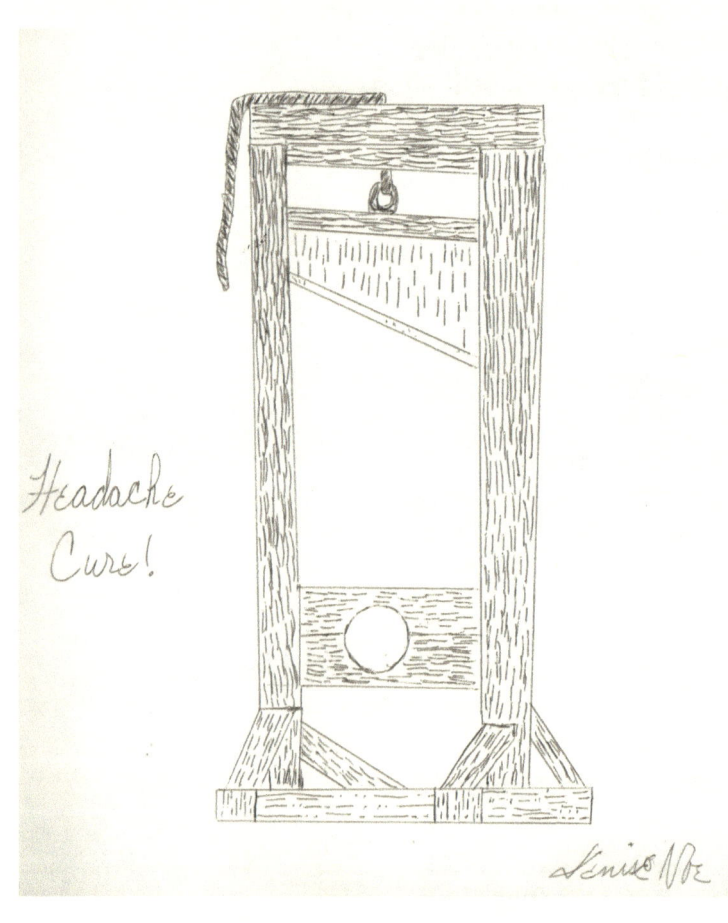

Headache Cure
Denise Noe

CHERITA

on second thought

maybe we shouldn't have
brought the children

to explore the haunted
Caves of Ceres where
those poor miners died

Lauren McBride

CHAINED SCI(NA)KU

moonflowers planted on
your grave
ghostly
white
at night
like you now

Lauren McBride

Aliens, Magic, and Monsters
By Lauren McBride

Fun to read. Fun to write. *Aliens, Magic, and Monsters* features poems set in the unlimited and imaginative realm of science fiction, fantasy, and horror. The poems were chosen to showcase over twenty poetic forms from acrostiku to zip, from strict rhyme to free verse, and much more in between. There are guidelines included on how to write each type of poem. Try a sci(na)ku. At only six words, it's sure to interest even the youngest readers.

Type: Juvenile and Young Adult Poetry Manual

Ordering links:
Print: https://www.hiraethsffh.com/product-page/aliens-magic-and-monsters-by-lauren-mcbride

ePub: https://www.hiraethsffh.com/product-page/aliens-magic-and-monsters-by-lauren-mcbride-2

PDF: https://www.hiraethsffh.com/product-page/aliens-magic-and-monsters-by-lauren-mcbride-1

FIBONACCI

FIBONOBSERVATION
James Ph. Kotsybar

Our
vast
cosmos
is watching
itself evolving,
orbiting to see the whole view
shimmering in millions of spotlights of sparkling stars.

JOINED FIBONACCI

they
find
it quite
easy to
follow the huge tracks
in the sandy planet's surface
until meeting the beast responsible for the tracks
and then find it quite difficult
to escape as the
beast devours
them one
by
one

    Guy Belleranti

JOINED SCIFAIKU

    first folding paper
    a folding flower
    in twilight

    he passed paper stars
    drove the paper airplane
    to mars

        Todd Hanks

TANKA

after bomb explodes
survive the nuclear blast
slow death from fallout
wires running out of you
power next-door neighbor's house

    Denny E. Marshall

from another world
flying rover lands by house
its long robot arm
firmly grabs you by the neck
drops you in sample basket

    Denny E. Marshall

ahead of time
strolling offworlders
smugly
misunderstanding notion
of human relativity

    Roxanne Barbour

under a tree
limbless bodies
and the worms
that feed on them
growing exponentially

    Christina Sng

we never knew
the intergalactic war
was right beside us
the cloak of darkness
across the Universe

    Christina Sng

HAIBUN

Superstitions

Bad luck bolted across the street, black tail gone in the snap of a whip. He swerves, changes course: thud, right turn, left, left again, and right, returning him to the other side of the avoided path but the car beside him proceeded on, crashed into a car that ran a red light—making me ask myself about picking up pennies, knocking on wood, the dent on his car.

    random gust
    a lily petal spins
    on a tombstone

Richard L. Matta

Sunset Through the Telescope

    Looking westward from the patio rooftop of the hotel, the sky is pale linen warming to luminous yellow voile above the seam line of a boulevard and a lacy selvage of green deciduous trees, the fabric of late July twilight.
    Walking past tables and lounge chairs, I wonder how the sky weaves its ever-changing colors, a felicitous twining of molecules and light.
At the edge of the building, a thin, bright-eyed man is happy to show me his prized reflecting telescope: The metal sleeve of black enamel and silver edging has a microscope-like eye piece attached along its side.
    Inside is an array of mirrors, he says.
    Cautiously, I bend to look through the lens and am startled to see the last rays of the setting sun vividly revealed at a ninety-degree angle, flattened as if I viewed film running through a projector,
a vision that excludes and estranges, forcing me to reconsider perspective, and how human vision clothes the world, providing the alluring but dangerous optical illusion that all revolves around us.

    the setting sun tucks in
    sideways behind the trees
    space station earth

Sandra J. Lindow

SILENT NIGHT

I glance at the chronometer above the broken control panel. It blinks once, twice, goes out. I slam it halfheartedly with my fist. It blinks again, stays on. It's set for Central Time so I'll always know what time it is back in Tulsa. Not that I can see Tulsa. Or Earth, for that matter. Not while floating somewhere in the Asteroid Belt, trapped in a life raft whose systems are failing. The chronometer reads 11:59 p.m. Seconds later, midnight. It is officially December 25th back home. I wonder what my wife is doing. Playing Santa and setting out presents for our little girl? Sitting on the front porch searching for me in the stars? And my daughter? Hopefully she's having sugar-plum dreams rather than lying awake wondering why Daddy never came home.

I suddenly want a Christmas tree.

I pull myself over to the parts bin. A pair of wire cutters, some spare 10-gauge wire, and my dwindling tube of epoxy, and in moments I have a six-inch, 2-D tree. I cut tiny ornaments from my tattered flight suit and affix them to the metal branches. But ... something's missing. I place my makeshift tree on the sill of the starboard portal, then shift my head just so. For a few seconds, distant Sol balances on the pointy tip of my creation, and my Christmas tree has a star. Tears pool in my eyes. I softly sing "Silent Night."

    drifting in an escape pod
    far from home
    my final Christmas

T. R. Jones

DRABBUN

Two Alone
Jan Cronos

Depressed, she didn't know what swam in filth under the woodwork, thinking dark, perverted thoughts. It was a horny scrawny rat alone inside a slimy hole. She also was alone, half-drowsing in an alcoholic daze.

As she wriggled in discomfort, the rusted springs of her sweat-stained mattress creaked in rodent speak whenever her fat behind weighed them down. The rat responded to that cry, which was a mating call, with ferocious squawking, but due to earbuds the woman didn't hear. And so, the rat crawled out his hole and into her bed.

> buck-toothed mouse
> nuzzling her nipples
> woman dreams delighted

Unseen
Randall Andrews

Ben was only four when he found the lamp, innocent and unaccountable for three poorly chosen wishes.

First came the bike, summoned from the aether by a snap of the genie's fingers. It was shiny and new and much too large for a child.

Next came the purple butterfly, which flew away the moment it came into being.
With his final wish, Ben asked for a special companion, the sort his preschool classmate claimed to have. But surely didn't. Not really.

It was by this wish that my tortured existence began—unseen.

    innocent wish made
    unintentional curse cast
    invisible friend

Through
Robert E. Porter

In 2016, Chip Taulbee interviewed bestselling *Martian* author Andy Weir for the *Mensa Bulletin*. Weir shared three tips for writers.

One:

"It's easy to sit around and imagine how awesome your story is going to be," said Weir, "but when you actually sit down and try to put the words into your word processor, that's when you find all the problems and the mistakes, and that's when it starts to be hard work." (Taulbee)

Writing is rewriting – until you get it right. That's good stuff. It's what separates writers from wannabes.

Two:

"[R]esist the urge to tell your friends and family about your story," said Weir. (Taulbee)

That also bears repeating.

Decades ago, Ray Bradbury gave SF writer Henry Kuttner credit for this advice:

> "Shut up," he said.
> "I beg pardon?"
> "You're always running around, grabbing people's elbows, pulling their lapels, shouting your ideas," Kuttner replied. "You give away all your steam. No wonder you never finish your stories. You talk them all out. Shut up."
> And shut up I did.
> (Bradbury)

It's important to finish our stories before sharing

them with others. But how, exactly? And for how much?

This brings us to Weir's final piece of advice:

"Now with eBooks and their continued popularity, there is no longer an old-boy network between you and your readers," said Weir. "You can write a book, put it up for sale, and suddenly millions and millions of people have access to it, and if they like it they'll recommend it to each other." (Taulbee)

Self-publish?

It worked for Weir!

A man-bites-dog story. I suspect a pre-existing condition. Weir, a successful tech wizard, put a spell over gamers? Their massed support greased the wheels, easing Weir's transition into publishing's old-boy network? After all, it wasn't his self-published edition that made the best seller list. And the adaptation to film was no indie, shoe-string budgeted Cinderella story. *The Martian* cost over a hundred million dollars to make -- a blue-chip investment, with Ridley Scott at the helm and Matt Damon, one of Hollywood's most recognizable faces, for their bubble-helmed poster boy.

You'll find a more likely self-publishing success story in the 2 January 2022 issue of the *Idaho Press*:

> *The caller was looking for her son's handwritten book, "The Adventures of Dillon's Crismis, by Dillon His Self." Dillon's book is an impressive 88 pages, complete with full-color illustrations and even a homemade library spine label, which came in handy when librarians had to locate it for his mom to come "check out."*
> (Staff)

It's newsworthy because the Boise-area self-publisher was only eight-years-old. If he had been forty-eight, and his elderly mother called up the library, who's going to know?

E-books! They're like snowflakes in a blizzard. How can you get anyone to grab yours, specifically? That's the problem.

As the Joshua Bell experiment illustrated, context is key. Gene Weingarten covered this story for the Washington Post. Here's my Cliff Bar version:

Bell, a professional musician, went from selling out a Boston theater at $100 per seat to busking in a DC Metro station. The same music, the same musician, the same million-dollar violin -- a change of venue, that's all. At the station, they valued his playing at... about $34. (Weingarten)

The moral:

The plant out of place gets treated like a weed.

Go play your theremin outside a Roger Starbucks or Flash Gordon food service. Who's going to stop you? But try playing "live" at Carnegie Hall, or opening for Boston. Musicians have to be selected for that. Curated, like a Ming vase or the merciless Piltdown man. There's a vetting process. People at those venues invest their own time, money, and talent. They sell certain expectations to the public, banking on those expectations being consistently met by the performers they have engaged. They all pull together, each one doing what he can to supply a known and existing demand. When it works, that's good business. They stay afloat.

Play beautiful music in a workaday location, however, or self-publish the world's best SF novel without a ready audience, and it should come as no surprise. Whatever they expected, whatever they have been demanding, it wasn't *this*. So, your effort and genius will go largely ignored. And what's that worth?

As much as a mother robin's lullaby or a squirrel's heartache.

And where does that leave us, dear reader? If you have come this far, it goes without saying. But I'll say it, anyway -- for those scribbling in the margins, or listening from the wings with egg on their faces:

"Aha!"

The point and purpose of ku? To disengage from the anxious, buzzing noise inside your head and become more fully engaged, if only for a moment. That's when you might hear the lullaby, or even feel for the tree-hugging rodent.

In hindsight, there are no captured moments. Each one is fleeting and priceless, to be embraced for its own sake before it slips away. The ku is not a fly in amber but a severed finger left behind -- pointing something out to those of us being covered in sap and showing us the way. The only way out is through.

WORKS CITED

Bradbury, Ray. "Introduction: Henry Kuttner -- a Neglected Master." *The Best of Henry Kuttner*. Ballentine Books, 1975.

Staff, Idaho Press. "Local boy self-publishes, secretly adds homemade book to library shelves." *Idaho Press*, 2 Jan 2022.

Strickland, Ashley et al. "New US Dietary Guidelines Include Babies and Toddlers for First Time." *CNN*, 30 Dec 2020.

Taulbee, Chip. "The Martian Calls: an interview with Sci-Fi Writer Andy Weir." *Mensa Bulletin*, February 2016.

Weingarten, Gene. "Pearls Before Breakfast." *Washington Post*, 8 April 2007.

A Bag Full of Eyes
By Robert J. Krog

In a kingdom haunted by witches, where vampires hunt in the night, when there are murders but not witnesses, when the method of murder reveals the how but not the who, one calls upon the eye-man to help solve crimes. The eye-man has the answer. It can be found in a bag full of eyes, along with things one does not seek. Thus the tale of Royal Inspector Sir Gordon.

https://www.hiraethsffh.com/product-page/a-bag-full-of-eyes-by-robert-j-krog

FEATURED POET: Joshua St. Claire

plum tree automatons
at the base of each trunk
"petal reset button"

beta testing
the lovebot's pleasure program
iambic pentameter

our long love's day
another life extension treatment
fails

black hole
crossing the event horizon
we begin again

Cheshire moon
a door opens
to another world

last kiss
the doctors begin
her brain download

Proxima Centauri
so close
I could touch it

many worlds interpretation
we discuss politics
around the dinner table

grafting scars
the cyborg forgets
the feel of flesh on flesh

black holes
threaded on the ecliptic
rosary beads

Rigel and Betelguese
the bright eyes
of a possum

heat death of the universe
each night
one fewer firefly

newborn
we all take turns holding
the first Martian

HORRORKU

freshly turned earth muffled screams

waning gibbous
changing incisors
in a changing jaw

Black Moon
no one knew
until the thaw

now you know
I really meant it
woodchipper

sea cucumber
how difficult putting
my insides back in

ghost crab
the agony inside
my shed skin

laundromat
the blood stains
just won't wash out

Joshua St. Claire is an accountant who works as a corporate controller in rural Pennsylvania, where he lives with his wife, three sons, and two cats. His poetry has appeared in journals in North America, Europe, Asia, and Oceania. His work in haiku and related forms has appeared in journals like Scifaikuest, The Heron's Nest, Mayfly, seashores, Sonic Boom, and Kokako as well as the Haiku Path at Monte Sano State Park. He has been nominated several times for the Pushcart Prize and Best of the Net. His work was included in the 2022 Dwarf Stars Anthology, and he is the first place winner of the Haiku Society of America's 2022 Gerald Brady Memorial Senryu Award.

INTERVIEW WITH FEATURED POET
Joshua St. Claire

How long have you been writing poetry?
I dabbled in poetry in my youth, writing poetry occasionally until about age 20, around the change of the millennium, when a period of pervasive writer's block set in. Fortunately, the muses began speaking again around 2019. I am very pleased to say that I am a teri santitoro discovery. My first accepted work was published in Scifaikuest.

Did you begin writing haiku before you branched out to scifaiku?
My journey with Japanese forms begins with scifaiku. I was experimenting with and researching formal poetry types when I stumbled across Scifaiku and thought...I think I can do this! From there, I branched out to mainstream haiku as well as postku, tanka, rengay, renku, and haibun.

How did you learn about scifaiku?
A google search for poetry types brought me to Scifaikuest. Further research led me to other fine journals like Star*Line, the Starlight Scifaiku Review, and Dreams and Nightmares which were foundational for me. Much of my learning comes through reading.

Where did you learn to write scifaiku?
I recommend Minimalism. It is an excellent resource for poets at any stage of their journey. Excellent scifaiku have, at their heart, an imagistic

juxtaposition. Once a poet understands this, any other learning is just gravy.

Do you write poetry other than genre poetry? If so, what kind?
I continue to be surprised to find that I have strong formal tendencies in my poetry. In addition to working in Japanese forms, I also frequently work in other fixed forms, particularly ghazal, villanelle, sestina, and rondeau. Learning the imagistic nature of Japanese forms, strongly changed my style and enhanced my other work.

Whose poetry has influenced you the most?
In order not to leave anyone out, I will limit myself to poets who have stopped writing: Sappho, John of Patmos, Nostradamus, William Shakespeare, John Donne, Andrew Marvell, Matsuo Basho, Alfred Lord Tennyson, Edgar Allen Poe, Gerard Manley Hopkins, Charles Algernon Swinburne, Christina Rossetti, W. B. Yeats, H.D., Wilfred Owen, T. S. Eliot, J. R. R. Tolkien, W. H. Auden, Wallace Stevens, Edna St. Vincent Millay, Jack Kerouac, Sylvia Plath, Jane Reichhold, and Marlene Mountain

Who is your favorite poet?
It depends on the day. It hard to find a better book than: T. S. Eliot's The Waste Land, John Donne's Songs and Sonnets, or Sylvia Plath's Ariel. There is quite a bit of the speculative in these poets' work. For instance, you might be surprised about how many times Plath actually wrote about dryads! I also enjoy any Contemporary English Language Haiku journals that I pick up.

What/who is your main inspiration?
Of course, speculative tropes and also: Christian philosophy and history, transhumanism, quantum

and particle physics, 90's alternative and grunge music, pop culture, the Western Canon, bodily integrity, illness, my childhood and family, plants, particularly flowers, the Anthropocene, Japanese Aesthetics, and fixed forms. I am sure this seems like a motley crew of influences, but I am sure, as any poet digs deep, they will also find a variety of disparate sources of inspiration.

I find it strange that I write very little love poetry. Since much of my writing comes from, frankly, disappointment and negative feelings, I suppose it's no surprise that this is the case because my wife and I have a wonderful, happy relationship.

What poetry magazines do you read/contribute to?
I read widely and broadly. I encourage others to do so as well! I have contributed to journals in North America, Europe, Asia, and Oceania. The full list would be too long to include here.
I have not found a journal dedicated to Japanese forms that I haven't liked. They range in quality from very good to excellent. I have been in many of them.
Beyond Scifaikuest, there are several speculative journals that I have contributed to and have an enormous amount of respect for:

    Dreams & Nightmares
    Eccentric Orbits Anthology Series
    The Flying Saucer Poetry Review
    Kaidankai: Ghost and Supernatural Stories
    Otoroshi
    Scifaikuest
    Shoreline of Infinity
    The Space Cadet Science Fiction Review
    Star*Line

FAVORITE POEM
by editor **t.santitoro**

I usually pick a scifaiku or tanka for my favorite poem. The poems below are the contenders for this issue's favorite:

leaving Earth --
our ancestors
failed us

Scifaiku by Michael P Coglan

snakes in the cockpit
specters in the cargo hold
space sickness is real

Randall Andrews

scrubbing rust
I stroke the cheek
that still feels

Tyler McIntosh

love letters
inscribed on my exes' skin
returned unopened

David C. Kopaska-Merkel

Yes, all of the poems above have wonderful ah-ha moments, and are wonderfully concise. They are all excellent poems. But my very FAVORITE this time is actually a haibun!

TR Jones haibun Silent Night *Moved me to tears! (Me, too. I knew as soon as I read it that this would be her choice. Managing Editor).*

Who?

Randall Andrews is a speculative fiction writer and poet from southern Michigan. When not writing, he can be found wearing the soles off a pair of running shoes, listening to his favorite John Williams soundtracks, or hand-feeding his loyal flock of wild songbirds.

Daniel Barlekamp is a poet and fiction writer who lives with his wife just north of Boston, Massachusetts. When he is not reading or writing, Daniel works as an immigration paralegal and attends law school in the evenings. He and his wife enjoy listening to 45s, exploring historic cemeteries, and playing with their cat and rabbit.

Brian Barnett is the author of the middle grade novellas Graveyard Scavenger Hunt and Chaos at the Carnival. He has over three hundred publishing credits in dozens of magazines and anthologies such as the Lovecraft eZine, Spaceports & Spidersilk, Scifaikuest, and Three Line Poetry.

Michael P Coglan is an all around nerd and haiku poet. He lives in Iowa with his wife and two dogs, Ripley and Gimli

Jenelle Clausen lives in Madison, Wisconsin, where she writes Medicaid publications by day and poetry by night. Her poetry has appeared in various literary journals.

Stephen Curro hails from Windsor, Colorado. Along with Scifaikuest, his short fiction and poetry has appeared in The Fifth Di... and Daily Science Fiction, among other venues. His sci-fi novelette The Spark is also available through Hiraeth Publishing. In addition to speculative fiction and poetry, Stephen writes educational materials for the nonprofit Taproot Guru. When he isn't writing, he works as a high school paraprofessional. When he isn't working, he enjoys scuba diving and plotting to trick his dad into watching Lord of the Rings. You can keep up with his shenanigans at www.stephenccurro.com.

Lorelyn De la Cruz Arevalo: I am member of the Write Your Legacy community in the Philippines, working as a medical transcriptionist in Singapore. I am also a self-published author of Twin deLights, "Haikuna Matata (a haiku collection) and Hainaku! It's Pundemic! I am Balot. Acovida dito." My works have been featured in some poetry/haiku journals and anthologies.

Greg Fewer: A lifelong fan of speculative fiction, movies and television, Greg Fewer is a former enthusiast of role-playing games (for which he has one scenario publishing credit), and writes predominantly flash fiction and poetry. His stories and poems have appeared in (among other places): Cough Syrup, Lovecraftiana, Monsters: A Dark Drabbles Anthology, Page & Spine, Polar Borealis, Scifaikuest, Star*Line, and The Sirens Call.

T. R. Jones lives in northern Texas, where he writes both mainstream and genre prose and poetry. His work has appeared in Lalitamba, Scifaikuest, Spaceports & Spidersilk, Star*Line, and Illumen. He is a member of the Society of Children's Book Writers and Illustrators and the Science Fiction and Fantasy Poetry Association.

Deborah Karl-Brandt, lives in Bonn with her husband, two rabbits and numerous books. After her PhD studies in Scandinavian languages and literatures, she works as a freelance author and poet. Her poems have been widely published.

Simon Kewin is the author of over 100 published short and flash stories. His works have appeared in Analog, Nature, Daily Science Fiction and many more. He is also the author of the Cloven Land fantasy trilogy, cyberpunk thriller The Genehunter, steampunk Gormenghast saga Engn, the Triple Stars sci/fi trilogy and the Office of the Witchfinder General books, published by Elsewhen Press. In 2022, he was an SPSFC semi-finalist and had a short story shortlisted for a Utopia award. He lives deep in the English countryside. Find him at simonkewin.co.uk and at @SimonKewin on Twitter.

David C. Kopaska-Merkel, a retired paleontologist, won the 2006 Rhysling award for best long poem (collaboration with Kendall Evans), and edits *Dreams & Nightmares* magazine (since 1986). He has edited *Star*line*, an issue of *Eye To The Telescope*, and several *Rhysling* anthologies, has

served as SFPA president, and is an SFPA Grandmaster. His poems (more than 1200 of them) have been published in *Asimov's*, *Strange Horizons*, and more than 200 other venues. ***Some Disassembly Required***, his latest poetry collection, comes out in 2022 from Diminuendo Press. @DavidKM on twitter.
Blog: https://dreamsandnightmaresmagazine.blogspot.com/

Dylan Mabe is an Appalachian writer with a deep love for sci-fi, fantasy, and poetry. He is currently studying Shakespeare in Staunton Virginia and acting as a member of the Treehouse Shakespeare Ensemble. Dylan would like to acknowledge that he is a white man writing in a form that Japanese culture and artists shaped for centuries. All reverence for the form lies with the early and modern Japanese artists that continue to revolutionize short form poetry.

Richard L. Matta was raised in New York's Hudson Valley, worked as a forensic scientist,
and is active in the San Diego poetry community. When not catering to his golden-doodle
dog, Elliott, he is active on the San Diego Bay sailing and fishing, hikes in the local area,
and volunteers in Balboa Park. He writes many forms of poetry, often addressing issues
of social concern in his work.

Josh Maybrook is a poet and speculative fiction writer inspired by history, mythology, and folklore. When he is not writing, he can be found browsing second-hand bookshops in search of new acquisitions for his ever-expanding hoard.

Lauren McBride finds inspiration in faith, family, nature, science and membership in the SFPA. Nominated for the Best of the Net, Rhysling and Dwarf Stars Awards, her poetry has appeared in dozens of publications including Asimov's, Dreams & Nightmares, and Fantasy & Science Fiction. She enjoys swimming, gardening, baking, reading, writing and knitting scarves for our troops.

Tyler McIntosh was born and raised where the mountains meet the valley to the south of Jackson, Wyoming. He is an environmental scientist, skier, and map-lover now based out of Colorado.

Ngo Binh Anh Khoa is a teacher of English in Ho Chi Minh City, Vietnam. In his free time, he enjoys daydreaming and writing dark verses for entertainment. His poems have appeared in Scifaikuest, Weirdbook, Star*Line, Spectral Realms and other venues.

Christina Nordlander was born in Sweden in 1982, but met a very nice English man and now lives with him outside Birmingham with two cats. She has been writing obsessively since childhood, primarily on the spectrum of dark fantasy - SF - horror. She also has a PhD in Classics and Ancient History from the University of Manchester.

Brian Rosenberger lives in a cellar in Marietta, GA and writes by the light of captured fireflies. He is the author of As the Worm Turns and three poetry collections - Poems That Go Splat, And For My Next Trick..., and Scream for Me.
https://www.facebook.com/BrianWhoSuffers
https://www.instagram.com/brianwhosuffers

Ronnie Smart is a New Zealand poet and writer of short dark fiction, who has been published in a range of literary and genre publications. He loves writing formal poetry, can communicate in Chinese, and can fight with a sabre.

Gabriel Smithwilson can assure you, that as you first read this, Ghostbusters is playing on a TV, somewhere in his apartment.

Lee Strong, OFS, is a husband, father, and dog dad who lives in Western New York, where he keeps watching the skies.

DJ Tyrer dwells on the northern shore of the Thames estuary, close to the world's longest pleasure pier in the decaying seaside resort of Southend-on-Sea, and is the person behind *Atlantean Publishing*. They have been published in *The Rhysling Anthology* 2016, Speculations III, and issues of Enchanted Conversation, The Horrorzine, Red Planet, Scifaikuest, Sirens Call, Spectral Realms, Star*Line, and Tigershark.
DJ Tyrer's website is at
https://djtyrer.blogspot.co.uk/

www.ingramcontent.com/pod-product-compliance
Lightning Source LLC
LaVergne TN
LVHW041635070526
838199LV00052B/3371